Jonestown Lullaby

Jonestown Lullaby

Poems and Pictures

Teri Buford O'Shea

iUniverse, Inc.
Bloomington

Jonestown Lullaby
Poems and Pictures

iUniverse books may be ordered through booksellers or by contacting:

iUniverse
1663 Liberty Drive
Bloomington, IN 47403
www.iuniverse.com
1-800-Authors (1-800-288-4677)

Because of the dynamic nature of the Internet, any web addresses or links contained in this book may have changed since publication and may no longer be valid. The views expressed in this work are solely those of the author and do not necessarily reflect the views of the publisher, and the publisher hereby disclaims any responsibility for them.

Any people depicted in stock imagery provided by Thinkstock are models, and such images are being used for illustrative purposes only.

Certain stock imagery © Thinkstock.

ISBN: 978-1-4620-3737-7 (sc)
ISBN: 978-1-4620-3738-4 (e)

Printed in the United States of America

iUniverse rev. date: 8/22/2011

Cover design by Paradise Copies, Northampton, MA
Photos courtesy of California Historical Society

This book is dedicated to my daughter, Vita,
who endured my struggles over the years;
to Martha, my lifelong friend, who showed me that
one person can make a difference;
and to Dan, who taught me to live with courage.

In memory of Judy, whom I loved as a sister.

Acknowledgements

With deep love and respect for the people of Jonestown, whom I shall hold ever in my heart.

With appreciation to all those who helped me see this book through to fruition. Heather Johnson provided invaluable editorial services. Saundra Dubow Azmitia, Rebecca Moore, Alice Bowen, Fielding McGehee III (Mac), Don Beck, Anne Adams, Joyce Anderson, Susan Roth, and members of the Florence Poets' Society provided generous feedback and encouragement.

With gratitude to Patrice who challenged me to live beyond the boundaries of survival.

This book was made possible, in part, by a grant from the Western Massachusetts Training Consortium "Career Initiatives Program".

…we with our spirit, our love, our sinew
we are among the survivors
spread the news.

-Fay Chiang
"In the City of Contradictions"

Contents

I Write

I write from the poor side of silence
Of an unholy priesthood that
Captured my soul for a time

These poems
Neither confession nor biography
Follow the voyage of a lonely spirit
Into a realm where there are no answers

Teri Buford O'Shea

About *JONESTOWN LULLABY*

When you read Teri O'Shea's poems in Jonestown Lullaby, you will be taken on a journey of intense emotion. Written over the years on scraps of paper, in journals, hidden away and later found by her daughter, these poems have been a long time coming into the light.

Stark, raw and powerful, O'Shea's poems are about survival---not just survival in Jonestown itself, but survival of the tremendous loss in its wake. The poems give us a glimpse of the secretive, fearful and bewildering world from which O'Shea escaped a few weeks before the massacre in Jonestown. Her poetry conveys unimaginable fear as well as enormous loss and despair, portraying the reverberations of the trauma of Jonestown in a new generation. Yet O'Shea's poetry also gives voice to the healing in friendship, in forgiveness, and in hope for new beginnings.

In addition to losing the community of people she lived with, worked with, loved and cared about, O'Shea had to face in isolation the terrible guilt of being a survivor. She was compelled to conceal her past due to the significant stigma associated with Peoples Temple and Jonestown. She, like other survivors, encountered disbelief, fear, even loss of employment, when she revealed she was a Jonestown survivor. As a result, she told very few people about having been a member of Peoples Temple. For years after her escape, O'Shea feared for her life because of her defection and lived in hiding. Only in the last several years has she come out publicly as a survivor.

It is no small act of courage to deal with the stigma, fear, loss, guilt and shame associated with being a Jonestown survivor and to reveal your own identity as a survivor and the dark places where you have been. It's especially hard when the media has reduced your experience to sensational headlines and most of what persists in popular memory are photographs of dead bodies in the jungle, the demonization of Jim Jones and jokes about drinking Kool-Aid.

The poems and photographs in Jonestown Lullaby demand that we remember more than headlines and images of bodies; they demand we remember that those who died were friends and family members who lived, worked, loved and played, and are still mourned. Jonestown Lullaby insists we acknowledge that the story of Peoples Temple and Jonestown is complex and multilayered; it did not end with the massacre on November 18, 1978, but continues to this day.

Heather Johnson
April 2011

About the Author

I first met Teri O'Shea in 1980 – two years after the Jonestown massacre.

Although we were both living in New York at the time, I had lived in San Francisco while the Temple was active there, and I had followed the stories about Jim Jones in the local papers.

When Teri first told me that she was a survivor of Jonestown, I did not know what to think. She was smart and funny, a graduate of U.C. Berkeley, a copy editor who loved a good pun. It did not seem possible that she could have been mixed up in the horrors that I had read about. She didn't like to talk about her experiences in the jungle, and it took many years for her story to unfold.

I gradually came to realize that she had lived through a situation filled with impossible contradictions. As Jones deteriorated, he demanded absolute loyalty to the community, but that meant he wanted his followers to betray each other. Jones preached love, but he would publicly humiliate people for minor infractions. In her final months in the Temple, Teri was under close surveillance because her most trusted friend had betrayed her when Teri tried to prevent a shipment of guns to Jonestown. To escape the jungle she had to pretend that she was leaving to work on the Temple's legal battles back in the states.

What leads a person to join an organization like Peoples Temple? Each person has a different story – in Teri's case, her childhood had been tumultuous. Since her father was in the Navy, the family had moved every two years. Teri was in nine different schools by the time she graduated high school - bouncing between such disparate places as Virginia, Ohio, Japan, Rhode Island, Norway, District of Columbia, and Pennsylvania. Her Appalachian mother, who struggled with mental illness, could not adjust to all the transitions; her father was often away at sea for long periods.

Teri left home at age 19 and found herself in California with no way to make a living. Like so many others living on the streets, she had trouble finding safe places to stay. The Temple offered her a home, a community, a job, and help with her college expenses.

Teri stayed in the Temple until age 26 – a total of seven years. Whenever I have asked her about why she stayed, she has talked about the community. She had smart, hard-working friends who held on to their dream of building a racially just community, even though they could see that Jones was deeply troubled. One of Teri's jobs was in the Jonestown School, and she loved the children, especially a little boy named Deitrick.

Many families had moved to Jonestown from dangerous ghettos in the U.S., and Teri was proud of the way those children blossomed in an environment where they could interact with exotic birds and wild monkeys instead of gangs. There was a lot of music in Jonestown, and one of Teri's best friends, Deanna, was a lead singer in the Jonestown Express band. The jungle itself was breath-taking, and Teri would often talk about the beautiful morning light or the sounds of the animals.

What is it like to be a survivor of a trauma like Jonestown? In these poems, Teri gives us a rare first-hand account of severe post-traumatic stress. A few of the poems are about the fragmentation she experiences in her daily life. A lot of them reflect the nightmares she has had every night for the past 33 years. In her dreams, she imagines conversations with people who died, or they rise from the dead to chase her. There are painful memories of Jones, such as the times he had people "rehearse" their so-called "mass suicide" or the time he held a gun to Teri's head to try to force her to say she loved him, and the moment of terror when she refused.

In other poems, Teri talks about piecing her life back together. There are fragments from her childhood, such as her visit to the ruins of Hiroshima while her father was stationed in Japan, and poems about the healing powers of friendship and childbirth.

Teri's poems remind us of the tremendous resilience of the human spirit. She has experienced more loss and pain than most of us can imagine, and yet she has survived and built a new life for herself. In the 33 years since Jonestown, she has had a career as a social worker, raised a child, and made new friends. Now, after three decades of silence, she has found the strength to publish these poems.

These poems are a wonderful gift from a woman who has a lot to teach us about survival. I thank Teri for her courage and her tenacity. Her life is a reminder that the human heart is stronger than we think.

Martha

A Friend Reflects: Sylvia

One day in 1974, I met a girl on a bus who was on her way to the first day of French class at Cal Berkeley, just like me. …She and I shared the same warm, steamy niche on that bus every day for a while, pressed in amongst the same 7:00 a.m. half-sleeping bodies.….

Now and then she would invite me to her church on Geary Street. But since I already had a church, I always declined. On that bus and on our daily walks up the hill.…we found ourselves to be soul sisters, sharing the same values – socialism, service, the end of suffering, peace. It was a year of idealism and pride for us, pride in what we already knew we would surely accomplish, pride in how we would one day change the world with our own hands.

I lost touch with my friend after that year. Then one day in 1978, I saw her again from a great distance. There she was on television, eyes haunted, gaunt, reflected on a backdrop of raw pain. Jonestown.

Jim Jones had surrounded himself with bright, beautiful young women, and she had been one of them. And she had survived, was still standing, even after the great hole had opened up in the world. But while she lived, nearly a thousand of those whom she had spoken of with such hope... had perished… I will never forget her eyes that 1978 day, flickering in black and white from across time and space, as long as I live...

In many ways, Jonestown reflects who all of us were, and could have been, in those days and in that place. We wanted the world to be fair, like all children do, and we had theories about how to make it so… Believing we were leaders, too often we were really followers, leaning to the simplest, loudest voice that promised the most. And in numbers, we were just so *many*, the largest generation of impressionable, idealistic, activist youth in our nation's history…

Jonestown. There but for the grace of God went each of us.

From *Rounding the Corner: Reflections on Writing About Jonestown*
by Sylvia Smith
http://jonestown.sdsu.edu/AboutJonestown/JonestownReport/
Volume11/SylviaSmith.htm

Teri Buford (left) Jonestown, December 1974. Photo by Claire Janaro.

A Brief History of Peoples Temple and Jonestown

Jim Jones founded Peoples Temple in Indianapolis, Indiana in the 1950s, as a congregation committed to racial integration. Working class whites and blacks came together to hear the gospel message of racial equality and social justice. Transcending their own prejudices and society's barriers, they worked together and worshipped together in the heart of Ku Klux Klan territory in Indiana. Eighty people—young and old, black and white—left Indiana and followed Jones to California when he prophesied that a nuclear holocaust would wipe out Chicago.

In California the group changed. It became more socially active and more engaged in local progressive politics. Jim Jones also changed. Jones asked his followers to call him "Father," or "Dad." He encouraged members to live communally, pooling their resources and donating them to church projects. And he began to see himself as divine, as the incarnation of Jesus or God, or as "God Almighty," as he declared to the congregation. He claimed to "heal the sick" and "raise the dead."

Life in the Temple in San Francisco was a mixture of long hours, self-criticism, musical entertainment, belly laughs, corporal punishment, and political activism. In other words, it was neither all good nor all bad. The group created a new, non-racist set of values:the word "black" indicated goodness, while the word "white" connoted bad, in contrast to the outside society's denigration of blackness. Mutual criticism sessions, called "catharsis," highlighted infractions members had committed. These ranged from making sexist remarks, to being irresponsible on the job, to stealing, to being caught with drugs, or to, the worst of all charges, being disloyal. The point of catharsis was to have the group change the individual, without resorting to the larger society's system of justice. There were stern physical and emotional consequences for such infractions.

In response to a number of events occurring in the United States, the Temple began seeking an outpost abroad, and in 1974 began clearing land in the Northwest District of Guyana, the only English-speaking country in South America. By 1976, the community had signed a lease with the government of Guyana, and had cleared thousands of acres. These Peoples Temple pioneers constructed barns, shelters, dorms, cottages, and all of the elements of a small town. But an influx of almost 1,000 Peoples Temple members arriving in 1977 overwhelmed the community and caused a number of problems for the developing infrastructure: sanitation, housing, education, electricity, health, and agriculture.

The move to the agricultural project, called Jonestown after its founder Jim Jones, saw the abandonment of almost all expressions of traditional religion. Progress reports and field notes replaced sermons; the Jonestown Express, a jazz band, replaced the gospel music of church with popular music of the day. And the same mixture of high communal spirits and dark paranoid fears pervaded the jungle community.

Opponents of Peoples Temple and of Jim Jones organized in order to repatriate their family members from Jonestown. Called the Concerned Relatives, the group put pressure on the media and on government officials to investigate Peoples Temple and Jones. Highly critical articles emerged in the press, and various investigations were conducted at the federal, state, and local levels. This external opposition led to increased internal repression in Jonestown, where dissent was equated with disloyalty. Day and night on loudspeakers, Jim Jones urged his followers to work harder and to beware of enemies. Loyalty tests occurred in Jonestown in the form of *White Nights*, or suicide drills in which people lined up to take poison, and practiced poisoning their children before taking the poison themselves.

A U.S. congressman arrived on November 17, 1978, to investigate conditions in Jonestown. Leo Ryan brought critical reporters and hostile relatives with him to the community. The visit went well until a few people asked to leave with the congressman's party. Fifteen left with Ryan and the reporters, followed a few minutes later by a truck with a few young men from Jonestown. When the group arrived at an airstrip six miles from Jonestown, these young men opened fire, killing Ryan, three reporters, and a Peoples Temple defector. They then returned to Jonestown where they found community members gathered in the central pavilion, listening to instructions from Jim Jones. Jonestown medical personnel surrounded a vat of fruit punch, laced with cyanide and tranquilizers. Jones exhorted the mothers to give the poison to their children and they did so.

Some protested, but were shouted down by some others in the group. Once the killings began, they apparently could not be stopped. Parents were forced to kill their children and then kill themselves. The shooters from the airstrip killed themselves. Jones was found shot to death. In all, 918 people died that day, of which 304 were children.

Part One
POEMS

Jonestown Lullaby

Sleep
Little children
Father
Loves you

White Night

Baboons howled in the jungle canopy
A dark night approached
The children were bedded down in their huts
Others exhausted from dawn to dusk work
Chatted among themselves
No star shined on this blackest of nights
"White night White night"
Jim Jones roared on the jungle loudspeaker
We were under attack
The end was near
Children and babies were pulled from their beds
Gunshots rang from the jungle's edge
Residents ran screaming to the Pavilion
"We WILL take our lives on this night in a
Revolutionary suicide" Jim Jones yelled
Two women passed out cups of cyanide-tainted Flavour-Aide
Some tried to run only to be stopped
By the gun wielding guards
Potion swallowed by all
We waited to die
Jim Jones laughed hysterically
"It's just a rehearsal"
He laughed again clapped his hands and said calmly
"Go home my darlings, sleep tight"

Revolution

Traitor!!
He roars
I shake
My knees
Turn to rubber
I collapse

My best friend
Shouts
I have abandoned
The Revolution

The Revolution
That creates
Despair
Hopelessness
Deprivation

The Revolution
That steals
My freedom
My self
My unborn child

The Revolution
That estranges me
From those I love and hold dear
That makes my best friend
My most feared enemy

My comrades
Grandstand
Against me
For His bemusement

I wonder who among them
Secretly wants
To leave too

The party line
The party line
The party lie

Truth
Buried somewhere
In the jungle floor
Far from
My reach
How much can it hurt
To tell

I clench my teeth
So as not to
Betray
Myself

I Do Not Love You

I do not love you
Like they think I should
No rapid heartbeat
No fireworks
No music in the air

Instead you point a gun
At my head
And command me to say
"I love you"
But I don't

I don't care
If you pull the trigger
This is the one thing
You cannot have

Bitter Jungle

Death cries from the bitter jungle
Blaming you for our
Fear, pain, horror
Collective cowardice

Believers we were
Trapped in your hypnotic thoughts
To live and die at your discretion

Afraid to rise up against you
Afraid your sorcery would destroy us
Blind to the power we held among us

We distrusted
Each other
Too much to save ourselves

I did not fight
I was not brave
I did not care if another day would come

You were not God
Not Buddha
Not Gandhi come back to life

Cries in the jungle night
Betray you now as never before

Forgiveness

You
      Familiar with
            Original pain
Squeezed my hand
      In one brave act
            Of forgiveness
So please
      Hold me gently
            In your soul
Teach me
      The lost art
            Of living
                  After death
      Has ruled
            So long

After the End of the World

After the end of the world
I drank milk, only milk
First in tiny sips
Then in large gulps
But it was only milk I had
After the end of the world

After the end of the world
I put the pieces of shattered glass
Together
And watched the sun rise
In its mosaic of reflections
Blue, rose, lavender
I heard the past talk
In silence

After the end of the world
I drove fast to nowhere
And nowhere
Became my home

After the end of the world
I now view the new sun set
Through my own screened porch
At the beginning of the world

Reflection

As I share my face with you
I long for a deeper acquaintance
I walk through quicksand silence
To the end of the world
And jump
Through madness into death

What the soul is
Nobody knows
An uncertain dream perhaps
The mind clinging to a space of its own
In search of a surly rapture
Simply to erase time

I slide out of the dark
Into the sun's buttery fingers
I share my face with you
So you can witness
Beauty unimaginable

I Could Not Be Trusted

It's not
That I could not be trusted
Never to heed the echoes of children
Torn from the living

Babies cooing
"Come with me"
"Hold me"
"Don't stay behind
While I die"
"Don't leave me
Alone in the ever after"

I could not be trusted
Not to listen

I could not be trusted
With the knife on the table

"I'm coming"

Spy

There was a shotgun in the closet
A guard dog by the door
A high-tech alarm system protected the house
But already
The informer was inside

Unremembered

I almost woke up
Without remembering
Those who had been denied their dignities
Reduced to the quintessence of pain
Exquisite and everlasting
Those who remain unremembered
Who died in no glory
Who fell backward into their graves
In the shadow of their own fear
Those who are now past all concern

As the sun rose
Their faces cascaded before my eyes
Never to be unremembered

Field Workers

Unblessed and unbelieving
Through the echoes of denial
They carry their world
With cutlasses over their shoulders

Lightning comes
Bleaching the sky of promise
Blurring the lines of choice
Swallowing up all decision

The field workers rise and fall
Yet have not lost their voice
Tired beyond strength
They make dire predictions

No longer strong
Each day collapses
Into a desperate search
For tomorrow

Unsacred Zone

Eyes hollow from the
Host of pills and syringes
He rules in an unsacred zone
Of paranoid secrecy
His messianic vision under siege

He claims to read my thoughts
Yet
Other voices, of no celestial urging,
Whisper to his abandoned mind

Dismal squawking on the jungle loudspeaker
Groan to the wind strange prophecies
Of approaching doom

Terror grows

I embark on a darker journey
Angry victim denounced for treason
I deliberate in the shadows
Beyond hope that words
Can cure his deadly mind

I plan my escape

My Angel

I pleaded to God
"Send an Angel
To save me"

From a distance
A woman slowly appeared
Through a thick curtain
Of cigarette smoke
Her frown silently screamed
"Go away!"

A yellow tank top
Barely covered her scrawny
Torso and shriveled breasts
On her wrist a gaping wound
That had bled until
There was nothing left
To bleed

Purple pop beads circled
Her long thin neck
As if to say she was
A woman of some culture
I said "Help me"
She flicked her cigarette ashes
And stared through me

Her long white hair moved slightly
With the jungle breeze
I ask again
"Will you save me?"
"Who will save me if not you?"
Coughing out a plume of smoke
She raised her arm
Pointed at me
Turned and disappeared

Terminal Breath

Sleep
A brief hiatus
Between paranoia
And the inexorable
Unveiling of truth
Yesterday's thoughts
Go best unremembered
Tomorrow's violations
Go best unforetold
A plan perhaps for
One terminal breath
Harkens escape
From the perverse pleasures
Of a madman

You Were Not Born

You were not born
To die
Like this

Flashback

I lose myself
In a vision of
What I once was

As I stand on this
Unholy ground
I shudder and try to
Find my way home

The address
I have forgotten
Keys were lost years ago

I walk to nowhere through
Surroundings ever so familiar

What will become

I light a cigarette
Don't smoke, never have

What door must I open
To extract myself from this
Soul-consuming process

Old friends speak but make no sound
I am an anachronism
Out of place, out of time

I panic, I know what's next
I'm lost in memory
With no way out

Midnight Tapestry

Bright and brief
As the fated star
Burning against the
Midnight tapestry
Streaming hot
Blue white trails
Into nothingness
Were your lives

Deitrick

"It's a baby animal book"

I sweep the dust
From under my bed
Back in the World

"I bought it for you"

I pack my lunch
For another day's work
Back in the World

"Can you say elephant?"

I search for my car keys
To go food shopping
Back in the World

"Touch the fuzzy duckling"

I order lunch
At the corner deli
Back in the World

"One, two, buckle my shoe"

I wash the day off
My face and hair
Back in the World

"I have a soft blanket for you"

I put on my reading glasses
And read a popular novel
Back in the World

"Come lie down. It's time to sleep"

I close my eyes
And remember
His lost smile

Grave Site

Stacked shoe-box style
Babies
Sandwiched in
Ground given grudgingly
To fast erase
Memory of the
Nameless

Silent shrieks
Do nothing to drown
Hell's chatter chatter
Relentless chatter

Mothers with dead wombs
Remember

Father
(aka Jim Jones)

Father
Crouching like a stranger
Hawking and coughing me up
Bits of me flying out in all directions
"You love your life too much"
He said, ending this terrible cleansing
"You won't be useful any more"
He expels me into waste water
Not in sickness but in disgust

Blue Moon

As the blue moon rises
Over the Jonestown compound
I secretly hide my hopes
Under tiny twigs
Beneath fallen branches

A gun tower looms above
In its shadow a strange man
With dark glasses and a hat
Whispers hauntingly

Wanna come with me?
Wanna come with me?
Wanna come with me?

Trembling, I follow
Leaving my dreams behind

Merge

Now
Before eternity and past
Merge in memory
I soothe my
Terror-ridden mind
With thoughts of you
Sleeping

Hiroshima Wall

Forever
Caught in one small gesture
A wave perhaps
Not as important then as now
Not as Keats would have it
With memories saved on a Grecian urn
One scald of light
One body spirited away
With such speed that it left
A shadow
Forever frozen
On this wall

Tall Grasses

I hold tightly to Mom
As we board
The flat-bottomed airboat
A gigantic fan at the back
Propels us across shallow water

We skim through
The tall grasses
Revealing the sweet-salty estuaries
Of the lower Mississippi Delta

A mosquito
Skips across the water
Landing on an old coca-cola bottle
Strewn disrespectfully into
What once was a pristine
Refuge for my family

I came here before
With Dad, Grandmother, Grandfather
All gone now
Yet the spark of
Their bright souls still
Glistens in the water's reflection

These green-blue waters
Beg me not to forget
My childhood laughter and joy
The angst of my teen years
Filled with sorrow and hope

We turn toward open water
Cut the engine…The boat jolts
Forcing me to hold
Even tighter to Mom
Lest she fall prematurely

The boat settles
I release my grip
And open a square box
Wrapped in brown paper
Tied with a string
Resting on my lap

The paper falls away
Unveiling a white Tupperware container
Reminding me of
The cookie-filled boxes
Mom made for school bake sales

I talk to Mom
About times past
And of future hope that
Flutters like a delta fish
In my expanding womb

I pull off the top of the box
A tear christens its contents
I lift my head
Tilt my hand
And release Mom
To the delta waters

Our family vigil thus honored
We head back through
The tall grasses
To what we once called home

In Your Enduring Presence
(In memory of Charles Buford Jr.)

At long last
We meet
Separated here by the mere
Mathematical perception of existence
I pay homage
To you
To your ancestors
To those who shared your vision

Mute in your enduring presence
I contemplate the task put to me
In this brief breath
Before I, too,
Succumb to my beginnings

I would that light flow backward
That matter become animate
Defying its natural structure
Breaking the bonds of time
I would that you were here now

For the moment
That you transcended the primal dust
You did honor to those before you

Homework

I met a girl in school
Who did her homework
Locked in the bathroom
Just like me
I asked to go to her house
"You can't" she said
"You can't come to my house either"
I replied

We both knew
We didn't have to ask

Time

Time
A river flowing
Through the years
Of our shared lives

Moments
Events that changed us
Rearranged us
Reshaped our existence

You
Lived the rule
That one person
Can
Make a difference

You saved me
From my past
Protected me
From myself
Prepared me
For the future

You found amazement
In the nuances of nature
With me, you shared
A joy of life
A satisfaction found
In a hard day's work
A belief
In the goodness of humankind

Time
A river winds
Between us
Carrying faith
That love and friendship
Endure

Haiku for Matt

I'll remember your
Gentle smile, your compassion
You made a difference

Birth

On a cold winter day
The nurse lays my
Newborn baby in my arms

Gently sleeping, a new life
Shines once more

I cradle you in my arms
I see your face
I call your name

Vita

You gurgle with
The joy of being

Harlem with Deanna W

Deanna
Exactly here
He stood
Then you
Singing to him
In his absence

Your song
Turned to tears
You rushed
To the street
Cursing the world
For its madness

Memories
Like sound waves
Oscillate, ricochet
Backward, forward
Converge again.
How perfectly
You and Malcolm
Harmonize
At the Audobon

Lest Their Dreams

Lightning comes
To those who seek thunder
Children talk to strangers
Though it may not be good for them
They learn fear from elders
Then refuse to sleep
Lest their dreams betray them

Anniversary Eve

RING RING

It rained today
Rain on snow
Only to refreeze on this night of
Deliverance

RING RING

Wanting contact with anyone
Willing to answer

RING RING

Please answer!
I need food
For my daughter's anger

Snow melts
On a rainy road
I can't reach you
Can't touch you

Cold fires
Do not burn hot
I speak rapidly
Seeking redemption

RING RING

Please answer!
I need food
For my daughter's anger

Their bodies
Have become ourselves
Inevitably seeking
Contact with the living
And pour old lies
Onto the burning snow

Tonight it's 17 degrees
White snow burns
On black ice

RING RING

On the Heels of Her Dreams

She has eyes like war
She sees the sun and moon forever starved
And does nothing
Her dead daughter tugs on the heels of her dreams
Sand shifts slowly under her cracked dry feet
She stands fast
Not giving in to
Hope

Broken Mirror

A broken mirror
Makes
Picasso-esque reflections
Of my face
A mosaic of memories
Shattered in time-
Less transitions of
A thousand screams

Life-lost children play
Laughing
Windless sounds
Into the sleepless ear
Of my daughter

Grieving

Grieving
Dry tears
A well dug
Beneath the
Riverbed
Kabuki rhythms
Survival pulse
One breath
At a time

My Daughter's Nightmare

This nightmare
Oozes
From your damp pillow
Carrying corrupt secrets
And
Lethal lies
Into your
Sleeping innocence

Struggling against its grasp
You run through the hall
Eyes open
Hair flying
Arms flailing
And

Bite me

Calm now
You take your
Blue-pajamaed self
Back to bed

Betrayal

We became
From the same darkness
Evolving, revolving
From humid heartbeats
Dreams, emotions
Memories we shared before words
Entered our imaginations

We lived
In a universe of hollow sounds
And deep echoes
Ideas yet without form

Today
The air heavy
With the thought of rain
Like tears held back
You silenced the primal rhythms
And broke the ancestral thread
Between   Us

Toucan Tanka*

Toucans' chatter call
My sleepy eyes awaken
Bright beaks beg for food

I share my morning breakfast
Fruit with my rainbow-faced guests

* Tanka is a poem with a distinct line and syllable pattern (5, 7, 5, 7, 7)

Fiction of Presence

A rupture of your usual trust
You truly thought I was delusional
Of course I wasn't a Jonestown survivor
You surmised

My hands trembled with fear
When I spilled my heart before you
Yet you questioned my intentions
Turned my memories into blasphemy
And chose not to believe
How I suffered all these years to exist

Somewhere behind your suspicions
You must have been profoundly frightened
So much so that you chose doubt over truth
Too convinced to check the facts yourself

Tears left no scars to prove my tale
Yet I am here... proof enough
I am not a fiction of presence

Part Two
PICTURES

Life in Jonestown

On the following pages are photographs of Peoples Temple members engaged in everyday life in Jonestown. Children are playing in a playground, elders are working in a garden, people of all ages are tilling fields, planting and harvesting crops, preparing food and eating together. The Jonestown settlers are young and old, black and white, friends and family members, doing activities common to community life.

These photographs, taken by Peoples Temple members, reveal an aspect of Jonestown rarely seen, at least not in the often sensationalized media coverage of Peoples Temple. They show that life for residents of Jonestown encompassed much more than the dark picture commonly portrayed. In spite of the hardships, the overcrowding, the long days of labor and struggle for agricultural self-sufficiency, many Peoples Temple members felt a sense of hope and expectation that Jonestown would become a community that exemplified social justice and racial equality. They worked hard to make it happen.

In a remote area of Guyana that was once only jungle, Peoples Temple pioneers cleared the land and constructed all the buildings for the settlement. They built roads and planted fields. Children went to school in one of the buildings and adult members taught classes; people took care of farm animals and participated in water brigades to irrigate the fields. Medically trained members provided health care to residents, delivered babies and even held clinics for local Guyanese neighbors. The Jonestown settlers also produced their own entertainment, putting on dance and musical performances. Young adults played on a successful basketball team.

These depictions of life in Jonestown do not deny the horrific deaths of 918 people, nor the terror, abuse and deprivation endured by many members. Rather, the photographs bring to light the neglected and complicated truth that life in Jonestown was more than the nightmare routinely portrayed in the media and more than what happened on its last day.

When you look closely at the individual Peoples Temple members in these photographs and see their smiles, laughter, pride, determination and camaraderie, you get a glimpse of the community many Peoples Temple members envisioned and strove hard to create.

H.J.

In memory of those who perished
in Guyana, November 18, 1978

Pictures

These Pioneers labored to build
Paradise
Deep in a South American jungle

Created from a powerful communion
Of sweat, love, hope and dreams
Utopia came to life
If only for a few fleeting moments

Now as my eyes
Behold these images
I remember
They never wanted
To become a memory

May we hold them ever
In the piety of our souls
As we seek our own
Healing and redemption

Teri Buford O'Shea

These photographs are printed with permission from the Peoples Temple Collection, California Historical Society.

Group of children with Peoples Temple members mid-1970's.

Planting crops, Jonestown, Guyana 1975 March.

Woman preparing food, Jonestown, Guyana 1977 November.

Woman working in fields, Jonestown Guyana 1977 November.

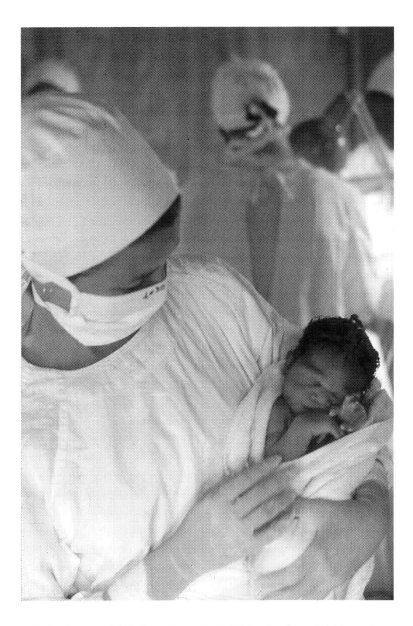

Judy Ijames with infant Camella Griffith, the first child born in Jonestown medical clinic, Jonestown, Guyana 1977 November.

Peoples Temple children in Jonestown, Guyana circa 1974-1978.

David Chaikin in garden, Jonestown, Guyana circa 1977-1978.

Tommie Keaton (right) with unidentified Peoples Temple member, holding eggs produced in Jonestown, Guyana circa 1977-1978.

Jim Jones (center), surrounded by Peoples Temple members, Jonestown,
Guyana circa 1974-1978.

Davis Solomen (standing) and other Peoples Temple members, Jonestown,
Guyana circa 1974-1978.

Virginia "Mom" Taylor, Jonestown, Guyana circa 1977-1978.

David "Pop" Jackson cleaning vegetables, Jonestown, Guyana
circa 1974-1978.

Workers loading onto truck, Jonestown, Guyana circa 1974-1978.

Cassava mill, Jonestown, Guyana circa 1974-1978.

Peoples Temple children, Jonestown, Guyana circa 1977-1978.

Peoples Temple members doing laundry, Jonestown, Guyana circa 1974-1978.

First arrivals to Jonestown clearing land, Jonestown, Guyana circa 1974.

Peoples Temple members working in fields, Jonestown, Guyana circa 1974-1978.

Peoples Temple children eating, Jonestown, Guyana circa 1974-1978.

Peoples Temple children working in fields, Jonestown, Guyana circa 1974-1978.

Peoples Temple members working in water brigade to irrigate crops,
Jonestown, Guyana circa 1974-1978.

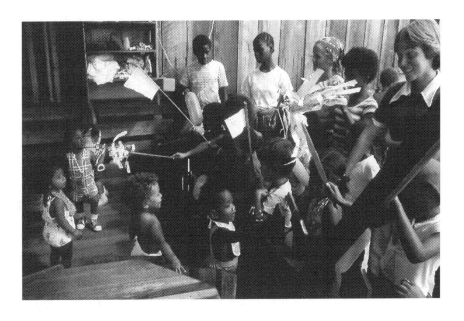

Children's nursery, Jonestown, Guyana circa 1974-1978.

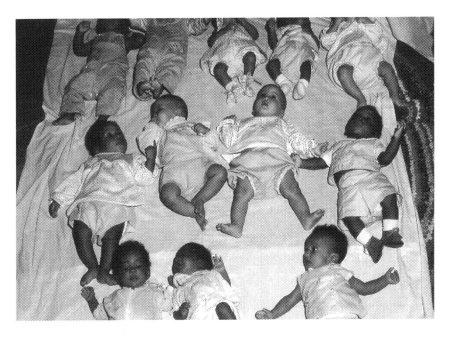

Infants in children's nursery, Jonestown, Guyana circa 1974-1978.

Peoples Temple children, Jonestown, Guyana circa 1974-1978.